THE PEER HELPER'S POCKETBOOK

Joan Sturkie & Valerie Gibson

Resource Publications, Inc.
San Jose, California

Editorial director: Kenneth Guentert
Managing editor: Elizabeth J. Asborno
Cover production: Huey Lee
Cover design: Jim Lizardi

Originally published as *The Peer Counselor's Pocket Book* © 1989 Resource Publications, Inc.

Resource Publications, Inc.
160 E. Virginia Street #290
San Jose, CA 95112-5876

Library of Congress Cataloging in Publication Data
Sturkie, Joan, 1932 -

    The peer helper's pocketbook / by Joan Sturkie and Valerie Gibson.

       p.   cm.

  Rev. ed. of: The peer counselor's pocket book.
  Includes bibliographical references.
  ISBN 0-89390-237-3

  1. Peer counseling—Handbooks, manuals, etc.
I. Gibson, Valerie. II. Sturkie, Joan, 1932-
Peer counselor's pocket book. III. Title.
BF637.C6S8 1992
158'.3—dc20   92-11052
                                    CIP

99 00 01 02 | 9 8 7 6

I dedicate this book to all of the peer helpers across the nation. This book is for you.
— *Joan*

I dedicate this book to my mother, Carol Gibson, for her love, understanding, and encouragement. She gave me the support to write this book (my first book!), and the ability to move forward in my life. Thank you, Mom, I love you with all of my heart.

And to my dad, Robert W. Gibson. You are my role model, and I'm extremely proud to be the daughter of such a distinguished writer. I love you. And to Esme, who is a special part of my life.

A special thought to Chris Gibson and Paula Gibson. Thank you for always being there when I need you and giving me "sibling" advice, which I treasure more than you know.

Also, thank you to all my special friends—you know who you are. And a very special dedication, in memory of Eric Seyler, a former peer counselor and a special human being.
— *Valerie*

CONTENTS

ACKNOWLEDGMENTS

We gratefully acknowledge the help of the following people:

Christopher R. Gibson — for the design and layout of the book.

Carol Gibson — for editing and giving suggestions.

James Lizardi — for designing the bookcover.

Jeff Cox, Rae Luce, and their peer counseling classes—for offering valuable input.

INTRODUCTION

Congratulations, you are now a peer helper! What exactly does that mean? It means you are a person who has been trained in communication skills, and you have learned how to apply them in helping another person with a personal or social problem. It also means you care about others and will take time to listen to their problems. Without giving advice, you will assist the person in managing and/or solving his or her own problems.

What responsibilities will you have?

1. To be available to the person needing help, whenever possible.

2. To listen.

3. To keep confidentiality.

4. To help the person solve his or her own problems.

5. To refer the person to a professional when warranted.

6. To report:

> **Child abuse** — to the department of social services or police.
>
> **Potential suicide or bodily harm** — to your leader, a professional, and/or a relative.

PURPOSE OF *THE PEER HELPER'S POCKETBOOK*

This book is written by a peer counselor and a peer counseling teacher/trainer to fill a frequently expressed need for a quick, easy-to-read reference. It is written to give you a handy guide which may be readily available (in your jacket pocket or purse) and easily referred to for information or review. Some of the material may be familiar to you, but remembering all of it without a reminder (such as this book) may be difficult. The purpose of *The Peer Helper's Pocketbook* is to make available to you a quick reference to reinforce those things which you learned but may have forgotten.

HOW TO USE *THE PEER HELPER'S POCKETBOOK*

Place this book in your backpack, purse, or pocket of the clothing you are wearing so you will have it available when needed. You may need it occasionally or frequently, but not having it with you might be the exact time you will need it.

Turn to the Table of Contents and check which chapter applies to your problem. Sub-headings are listed for your convenience. In Chapter Five spaces have been provided for you to add local telephone numbers as a referral service.

You will find this book to be most useful after you become thoroughly familiar with it and are able to find your answers quickly. We suggest you spend some time to fill in the telephone numbers and to become acquainted with the contents before you need the referral information.

CHAPTER 1

TIPS

RULES FOR HELPING PEERS

There are certain basic concepts you will always want to remember when you help a peer. These are generic in nature and will apply to any age person or any helping situation. Review these tips daily until you find you use them as automatically as you do your toothbrush. As with any skill, improvement will come with practice.

- Be nonjudgmental.

- Be empathetic.

- Do not give advice.

- Do not take responsibility for the other person's problem.

- Stick with the here and now.

- Do not argue, verbally or nonverbally.

- Listen between the lines.

- Deal with the feelings first.

- Be genuine and sincere.

- Keep confidentiality.

- Be a vital part of a caring network.

MEETING A STRANGER

Remember, some people who need your help the most will not be those who will ask for it; the person sitting alone at lunchtime or the one standing alone at a social gathering may be feeling very lonely. This person may need your care and understanding as much as any of your helpees. It will be up to you to reach out to the stranger. You may do this by introducing yourself, starting a conversation, and listening to what the other person has to say. By using active listening, you will probably discover his or her needs and may be able to initiate future meetings to continue the helping relationship.

Steps for meeting a stranger

1. Introduce yourself.

2. Initiate conversation which stems from the present surrounding and mutual interests.

3. Encourage the person to talk about himself or herself.

4. Be cautious about asking questions of a personal or intrusive nature. Show consideration for the person's privacy.

5. Listen attentively

6. Use open-ended questions, which usually begin with "How" or "What."

7. Show sincerity and respect to strangers.

8. Initiate appropriate closure, which may include exchanging phone numbers or making plans to meet again.

CHAPTER 2

SKILLS

The word "skill" may be defined as an ability which is gained by knowledge and practice. To work effectively as a peer helper, certain skills must be learned through this process. These skills are constantly improved and perfected as you put them to use.

Basic to all peer helping will be skills in developing active listening, responding to helpees, sending effective messages, practicing values clarification/problem solving/decision making, and intervening in a crisis.

DEVELOPING ACTIVE LISTENING SKILLS

Characteristics of Active Listening

- Restate the person's most important thoughts and feelings.

- Be attentive. Don't daydream—keep your thoughts from wandering. Focus your thoughts on the person you are listening to.

- Convey understanding and acceptance by non-verbal behavior (posture, voice tone, eye contact, facial expression, gestures).

- Put yourself in the other's place to understand what the person is saying, how he or she feels, and the values involved in the situation.

- Do not interrupt. Have patience—allow the person time to express his or her full thoughts and feelings.

- Do not offer advice or suggestions.

- Avoid bringing up similar feelings and problems from your own experience.

- Develop the attitude that listening is fun and personally enriching.

- React appropriately. Applaud with nods, smiles, comments, and encouragements.

- Do not argue mentally with self-talk.

- Have a desire to listen. There is no such thing as uninteresting people—only disinterested listeners!

- Do not antagonize the speaker with hasty judgments.

- Listen for camouflaged feelings. Many times feelings are hiding behind words. Ask yourself what feelings you think you are hearing.

- Avoid changing the subject. Sometimes you may get off-track and need to refocus on the actual issue.

RESPONDING TO HELPEES

- *Use open-ended questions.* Avoid questions requiring a "Yes" or "No" answer. Also remember to stay away from "Why" questions—these tend to put the helpee on the defensive. The helpee will feel the need to justify his or her behavior. Other words to beware of are "Did," "Have," and "Is." Good words to lead off a question with are "How" or "What."

- *Avoid making premature conclusions.* False assumptions invite erroneous conclusions.

- *Clarify the helpee's feelings, thoughts, and/or problems.* This will be helpful to both you and the helpee. Often the helpee needs to have what he or she has shared clarified. And sometimes it is important to have the helpee clarify something for you.

- *Focus on the helpee's feelings.* This shows you care about the helpee and offers validation of his or her feelings.

- *Do not be afraid to make a mistake.* It is O.K. to guess wrong about how the helpee feels or what he or she means. The helpee will appreciate your effort and attention.

- *Do not solve the helpee's problem.* It is important for the helpee to come to his or her own resolution. The helpee, through discovering his or her feelings and options, will be able to solve the problem himself or herself. In allowing the helpee this space, he or she will experience a feeling of adequacy and satisfaction.

- *Do not over-analyze.* This might cause the helpee to feel uncomfortable and to put up barriers.

- *Do not give "pat" answers.* Responses such as "Don't worry" or "Everyone goes through that" suggest what the person is feeling is unimportant. When someone is worried, he or she will not feel better after being told not to worry. If anything, the person will feel worse! It is necessary to validate, and help the person understand, his or her feelings.

- *Ask questions to help the helpee along.* Certain questions will aid the helpee to focus on the issue, look at it from a different perspective, and reveal information not already disclosed. In responding to your helpee, you might feel stumped on *how* to do it. What can you say after the helpee finishes talking? Some examples below might help you.

  → When asking questions:

    How are you feeling about that?
    or
    Can you tell me more about what happened?

  → When reflecting what the helpee shared:

*You seem angry about what they
said...*
or
You would like to see a change...

→ When conveying understanding:

This must be very difficult for you.
or
That can really hurt.

→ When clarifying:

*Are you saying it doesn't matter if
she leaves?*
or
*It sounds like you're afraid of what
they might do. Is that right?*

→ When summarizing:

*It sounds like you feel torn in the
situation. You want to live with
your Mom, but you don't want to
hurt your Dad's feelings.*

SENDING EFFECTIVE MESSAGES

Sending effective messages is important in peer helping, and it is equally important in personal relationships. Certain guidelines will help you as you practice this skill.

- Use "I" statements for expressing feelings. Remember to "own" your feelings.

    → A correct example: "I am angry with you because..."

    → An incorrect example: "You make me angry when you..."

- Be congruent with verbal and non-verbal messages. Your body language should match your words. An incongruent message is often confusing because the receiver must decide whether to pay attention to the verbal or the non-verbal message.

    → A congruent example: A person says he or she feels fine, while a smile is on his or her face.

    → An incongruent example: A person says he or she feels fine, and a look of pain is on his or her face.

- Communicate *caring* and *acceptance* of the receiver's feelings and reaction. Active listening may be used to respond to the receiver.

  → Examples: "I seem to be hearing you say the break-up with your boyfriend was not something you wanted. That must make it very painful."
  or
  "It sounds like you are in a lot of pain because of the unwanted break-up with your boyfriend."

- Be specific. "You always..." or "You never..." are generalizations. It is important to give someone an exact example of his or her behavior.

  → A correct example: "You cut classes four times last week."

  → An incorrect example: "You always cut classes."

- Include "want" statements in expressing what you would like someone to change. If the speaker does not convey explicit expectations in his or her message as to what is wanted, the receiver may perpetuate the personal dilemma, believing he or she is powerless to resolve the situation.

Asking Questions

In sending effective messages, there are three kinds of questions used in communication. These are: closed questions, open-ended questions, and "Why" questions.

- Closed questions ask for specific information, such as: "Did you go to the store?" This type of questioning discourages the person from talking. Closed questions usually begin with "Is," "Did," or "Have" and are usually answered with a "Yes" or "No."

- Open-ended questions encourage conversation because feelings are allowed to be discussed. The most effective questions begin with "How" or "What."

- "Why" questions should be used infrequently because they often put the receiver on the defensive. Sometimes "Why" questions make people feel they must explain or justify what has happened.

PRACTICING VALUES CLARIFICATION, PROBLEM SOLVING, AND DECISION MAKING

Values clarification, problem solving, and decision making are all interrelated.

Values Clarification

Listed below are some guidelines to consider in values clarification:

- Active listening assists helpees to express their feelings.

- Listen for what is important to the helpee.

- Restate to the helpee what you heard that seems important to him or her.

- Ask questions to aid the helpee in clarifying what is important to him or her.

- Assist the helpee to verbalize one or two values in respect to his or her problem.

- Brainstorm some other values.

Problem Solving and Decision Making Model

Ten steps are generally recognized in effective problem solving and decision making:

1. *Clarify feelings* — use active listening to assist the helpee sort out feelings. Making a list of these feelings may be helpful.

2. *Gather information* — find out as much as you possibly can about the situation.

3. *Define the problem* — what does the helpee perceive as the problem? Sometimes the first problem presented is not the primary one.

4. *Identify the decision* — what does he or she want to change?

5. *Brainstorm alternatives* — use open-ended, feeling-level questions to explore what the real problem may be.

6. *Evaluate the alternatives* — list all possible solutions. Have the helpee prioritize the solutions in order of importance. Brainstorm the pros and the cons.

7. *Predict consequences* — discuss the outcome for each possible decision.

8. *Clarify values* — will certain decisions violate the helpee's values?

    Example: "I will not ride with friends who are drinking and driving because I value my own life."

9. *Make an action plan* — list the things which must be done first, second, and third to carry out the decision. Assist the helpee to make a plan for completing each step in a given amount of time.

10. *Follow-up* — make an appointment for the helpee to see you again and to report how the decision is working out for him or her. If it is not working well, start over. Use the ten steps again and arrive at a different decision.

Clarifying Conflicts and Finding Resolutions

A conflict may be defined as a disagreement, dispute, or quarrel. Students have a variety of conflicts in their lives. As a peer helper, you will need to assist the helpee in recognizing and dealing with his or her conflict.

Conflicts may be internal, where the student is in conflict with himself or herself, or external, involving one or more people. The conflict also may be between a student and a collective entity, such as a school.

Conflicts may be resolved by:

1. Identifying the problem.

2. Listening to complaints.

3. Gathering information.

4. Seeking alternatives.

5. Making an action plan.

6. Reviewing the outcome.

INTERVENING IN A CRISIS

A crisis may be defined as a situation which arises and threatens one's psychological equilibrium. These life events or situations may be expected or unexpected, real or imagined, actual or potential. During a crisis, a person becomes very vulnerable because basic human balance is disturbed.

A crisis affects the physical body as well as the emotional being. It may be manifested in the form of:

-   sweaty hands

-   feeling faint

-   racing heart

- change of body temperature
- shock
- vomiting

Prolonged physical responses may include:

- chronic fatigue
- allergies
- sleeping disorders
- migraine headaches
- gastrointestinal disorders
- heart problems

Steps to follow when intervening in a crisis:

1. Provide the most appropriate level of protection, security, and nurturing, according to the person's obvious physical and mental needs.

2. Find out what the crisis is and what caused it.

3. Explore why the person cannot handle the current situation as he or she has done with other problems in the past.

4. Now that you know the problem, make certain the helpee also understands the situation and how it relates to him or her.

5. Explore alternative ways of coping with the problem and more positive ways of viewing the situation.

6. Lend appropriate support to the helpee's efforts at managing or resolving the problem.

7. Assist in the full recovery process toward a restored balance and/or an improved level of functioning.

Goals for helping someone with a crisis:

• Help the student cope effectively with the crisis situation and return to a normal state of functioning as soon as possible.

• Follow up after the crisis is over to see if the student is getting along satisfactorily.

The Chinese word for "crisis" involves two characters: one means danger; the other means opportunity. A student may see the crisis as a danger because he or she may be overwhelmed by the situation. It may also be viewed as an opportunity for the student to change and develop better ways of coping.

Remember: As with any skill, peer helping improves with practice.

CHAPTER 3

THE HELPER-HELPEE RELATIONSHIP

There are some essential elements involved in establishing and maintaining an honest, healthy helper-helpee relationship. These include: initiating contact with the helpee, defining your role in the relationship, establishing trust, and being aware of certain boundaries. Each of these should be considered. Be conscious of them—they are important!

INITIATING CONTACT

- Introduce yourself and let the helpee know you are a peer helper.

- Your first meeting with the helpee often feels uncomfortable—that is O.K. This awkwardness will decrease with time.

- If initially you have problems getting the helpee to talk or open up, share a

little about yourself. Talk about
whatever seems pertinent at the time.

DEFINING YOUR ROLE

- Ask why the helpee needs help. Why
  did he or she reach out to a peer helper?
  How does this person feel about
  working with you? Often the helpee
  will be nervous, and asking how he or
  she feels about the situation may help
  release some of the anxiety.

- State the kind of help you can offer,
  relative to the problem he or she has.

- State your desire to help and to be
  available for the person.

ESTABLISHING TRUST

- Assure the helpee of the confidentiality
  in the relationship. It is important,
  however, to let the helpee know there
  are particular things you need to report
  to authorities, such as child abuse or
  indications of a potential suicide or
  homicide.

- Discuss with the helpee how often you
  will meet. Beside the obvious necessity
  of arranging a time, this also reassures

the helpee someone is there for him or
her. This provides something consistent
in the helpee's life, and a dependable
friend.

BEING AWARE OF BOUNDARIES

- As in any relationship, there are
  boundaries over which neither party
  should cross. As peer helpers, you are
  there to *listen*. You should not intrude
  into certain areas of the helpee's life
  unless they have given you permission
  to do so.

- You have boundaries also, and it may
  be necessary to establish these with the
  helpee. It is important to keep in mind
  that you are not responsible for the
  helpee's actions or feelings. Never feel
  guilty if things do not turn out right for
  the helpee.

Things to Be Aware Of

Being aware of boundaries may also help to
prevent two different kinds of situations which
will jeopardize the helper-helpee relationship.
One of these situations occurs when the helper
becomes the "rescuer." Another difficult situation may occur if the helper and the helpee get

attached to each other and become emotionally involved.

Do Not Rescue

As a peer helper, your role is not to save the helpee. You are there to help the person help him- or herself. If you become a rescuer by taking care of something for the helpee, or by enabling him or her not to take risks, you are doing a disservice. You would cause harm to the helpee and his or her personal growth by assuming responsibilities which are not your own or by providing over-protection. In this respect, you would be violating a basic rule of peer helping.

The Danger of Getting Attached

Getting attached can go either way. The helpee may develop a desire to become closer to you, or vice-versa. The desire may also be mutual. If you find you get along with the helpee and want to become socially and/or personally in-volved, this is not necessarily wrong. But it is important for you to be aware that the helping relationship will be sacrificed. No longer will you be an objective person—the purpose and needs in the helping relationship will be clouded and displaced. You will have lost the emotional dis-tance between you and the helpee, which is essen-tial to being an effective peer helper.

Things to Remember

- If in the helper-helpee relationship stronger feelings become apparent, you must establish how you feel toward the helpee immediately. The helpee may need to work with a different peer helper.

- If you find the helpee is becoming too dependent upon you, reestablish your boundaries and talk with him or her about how you feel.

- When closing the helper-helpee relationship, review the progress the helpee has made. Assist the helpee in recognizing where he or she was when the helping relationship began and what has been accomplished since that time.

CHAPTER 4

SELF-AWARENESS

Self-awareness is a vital part of peer helping. Peer helping not only has to do with what the helpee is going through, but also with what is happening in your life. Being in touch with how you are feeling, or something you are experiencing, greatly affects how you can help a helpee. For example, if you have just had an argument with a friend and are now in a helping session, chances are the fight will affect your nonverbal and verbal communication. The helpee will be able to sense something is wrong. If you are still feeling frazzled from the argument, you will be unable to be there for your helpee in a healthy way.

In a situation like this, there are some things you can do before and during your session with the helpee:

- First, try to calm yourself and focus on your feelings.

- If there is time before you meet with your helpee, seek out a peer and talk about how you are feeling.

- If you are still feeling upset, let the helpee know where you are coming from. You may feel more comfortable after being honest with him or her. If you do not feel focused enough to be there for your helpee in a facilitative manner, ask the helpee if he or she would like to meet at another time. Sometimes this is not an option; at least communicate your feelings, thus allowing you to be less distracted with your problem and better able to be a good listener.

Peer helpers, by no means, are without problems. Everyone experiences pain in his or her life. Peer helpers are human too. Through experiencing and working out problems, peer helpers can listen more empathetically and be of greater value to the helpee. Your function is to be a caring, understanding listener. How can you do that if you are unhealthily internalizing and running from your feelings

When people keep their feelings in from family, friends, and helpees, those feelings get displaced. Be aware of what you are feeling and why. Be as honest as you can about your feelings—this will help prevent you from releasing your feelings in an inappropriate manner not only with a helpee, but with others as well.

Self-awareness is an integral part of peer helping for another important reason. Peer helpers are not "perfect"—they have problems too. If you are honest with yourself, sustain your self-awareness, and deal with your feelings, you will relate better to someone who is experiencing the same thing you did. For example, if you have a drinking problem and are in denial about it or not seeking help for yourself, you may run into a problem when a helpee approaches you and he or she has a drinking problem. You may not recognize that the helpee has a problem. If the helpee specifically requests guidance in that area, and you have not dealt with or accepted your own drinking problem, it is most likely you will not be clear-headed on the subject and able to give him or her the best information needed. Although, if you have recognized you have a problem and have sought help for yourself, you could be a tremendous help for your helpee. You will understand where he or she is coming from and be able to share your own experience. The helpee will know that he or she is not alone and help is available.

The above situation is only one example. In practicing self-awareness, there may be a whole array of problems to recognize and to resolve in your life: from school or work problems to serious family problems. It is very important to re-

solve those problems and deal with the feelings
in a responsible, healthy way.

HOW TO CHECK YOUR
SELF-AWARENESS

- Be honest with yourself and others. You
  may want to internalize your feelings
  and act as if everything is O.K., when
  really, it is not. This can be very
  dangerous and lead to emotional
  instability.

- Recognize your feelings. Focus on those
  feelings.

- Don't run from whatever you may
  discover. Talk to someone about what
  you are feeling and what is happening
  in your life.

- Listen to others and their input.

- Do not discount or minimize your
  feelings—any feeling is important and
  deserves validation.

- Once you have recognized those
  feelings, deal with them in a healthy
  way. This may include a number of
  things: for example, resolving an
  argument or bad feelings about
  someone, seeking help for yourself, or
  writing down your feelings for even

further release. The list is endless once you put your mind to it.

QUESTIONS TO ASK YOURSELF

There are questions you might consider asking yourself after meeting with a helpee. These questions may help you reflect on your session to discover areas of your skills which you may want to work on. It may also help shed some light on your helpee's problem and reveal how you can be most helpful to him or her.

Concerning Active Listening

- Did I focus solely on the helpee?

- How was my body language?

- Did I respond with appropriate nonverbal communication?

- Did I refrain from giving advice?

- Did I refrain from passing judgment?

- Did I allow the helpee time to completely express his or her thoughts and feelings?

- Did I restate (reflect) the helpee's feelings?

- Was I able to uncover feelings the helpee was hiding behind words?

- Was I empathetic?

- Did I put myself in the helpee's shoes to understand how he or she was feeling?

- Did we stick with the issue at hand?

- Did I refrain from arguing with the helpee?

- Was I supportive?

- Did I express caring and love?

Checking My Responses

- Did I validate the helpee's feelings?

- Was I able to ask questions which facilitated the helpee to further express his or her feelings?

- Did I do anything which caused the helpee to put up barriers?

- Did I avoid over-analyzing?

- Did I refrain from expressing my opinion?

- Did I use open-ended questions?

- Was I able to clarify and summarize the helpee's thoughts and feelings?

Examining the Helpee's Problem

- What feelings did the helpee express?

- What is the issue being dealt with?

- Is this a problem I need to report to the proper authorities? (If unsure, always check with your supervisor.)

- Did the helpee seem to feel better after the session?

- If we did not arrange another time to meet, do I need to try to meet with the helpee again?

General Questions

- Am I feeling guilty about something involving the helpee? (Remember—You are not responsible for the helpee's problems or feelings. *Never feel guilty.*)

- Am I comfortable with the problem the helpee needs to work on?

- Do my values get in the way of my objectivity on this particular issue?

- Do I need to discuss the helpee's problem with my supervisor?

- Does this problem require a referral?

- Do I have any irritating habits I need to change (interrupting, daydreaming, poor body language, etc.)?

- What can I do differently next time to better support and listen to a helpee?

CHAPTER 5

REFERRALS

You are trained and able to help peers, but there will be times when your helpee will need professional help. Do not feel inadequate when the situation is beyond your capabilities. You have already performed an important task by assisting the helpee in identifying the problem and in seeing the need for contacting another person. When you have accomplished this, you will then act as a "bridge" to professional help.

Remember to let your helpee know that you are still available for support while he or she is receiving additional help. It is also important to be available for the helpee when the outside help has been completed. The professional counselor may ask for your assistance after discharging the client. This help would come in the form of alerting the professional if things start to go downhill again for the student. This is particularly true of students who have previously attempted suicide.

WHEN TO REFER

As a peer helper, you should refer a helpee when you lack the skill/experience/ knowledge, emotional stamina, or time to begin or continue helping someone.

Seek outside help when your helpee is:

- requiring medical attention
- showing aggressive behavior
- abusing drugs
- talking about suicide
- being physically, sexually, or emotionally abused (child abuse)
- appearing to be emotionally unstable
- asking for professional help
- having a legal problem

If there is ever a question of whether to refer or not, ask for guidance from your peer helping teacher or the person supervising you. When in doubt, do not linger about making a decision. Check with someone immediately.

WHERE TO REFER

Peer helpers need to be familiar with agencies and persons in the community to whom they may refer their helpees. The list of referrals may include suicide prevention centers, physicians, Alcoholics Anonymous or other 12-Step programs, child abuse agencies, departments of public social services, psychiatrists, psychologists, and marriage, family and child counselors.

For your convenience, a list of some referral places are given below. You will need to write the local phone numbers on the lines provided.

Use this referral phone list when your helpee has a problem relating to:

AIDS

AIDS information (local)   _____

Hospital   _____

(Other)   _____

Alcoholism

Alcoholics Anonymous (local)   _____

Alateen, Alanon headquarters   _____

Alateen, Alanon (local)   _____

Chemical dependency hospital   _____

(Other)   _____

Child Abuse

Child Abuse Hotline   _____

Public Social Services
Department
(Child Welfare Office)   _____

Police   _____

(Other)   _____

Depression, anxiety, confusion

Mental health clinic   _____

Private psychiatrist,
psychologist, or licensed
counselor   _____

(Other)   _____

Drug Abuse

Alcoholics Anonymous (local)   _____

Narcotics Anonymous (local)   _____

Cocaine Anonymous (local)   _____

Drug abuse treatment center   _____

(Other)   _____

Eating Disorders

Overeaters Anonymous   _____

Private clinic   _____

Psychologist or other mental
health professional   _____

Anorexia and bulimia specialist   _____
(Other)   _____

Financial Matters

Local welfare office   _____
United Fund Office   _____
Local church   _____
(Other)   _____

Handicap

Society for the Blind   _____
Crippled Children's Society   _____
(Other)   _____

Legal Matters

Legal Aid Society   _____
Local attorney   _____
(Other)   _____

Marriage

Marriage, Family, and Child
Counselor (local)   _____
Psychologist or other mental
health professional   _____
Shelter for abused wives   _____
Local clergy   _____
(Other)   _____

Missing Person

Police Department   _____
(Other)   _____

Physical Illness

Doctor's office (local)   _____
Hospital (local)   _____
(Other)   _____

Poisoning

Poison Control Center   _____
(Other)   _____

Pregnancy

Doctor's office (local)   _____
Community clinic (local)   _____
Home for unwed mothers   _____
Social Services Department   _____
(Other)   _____

Rape

Rape Hotline   _____
Hospital   _____
Police   _____
Mental health professional   _____
(Other)   _____

Spiritual or Religious Needs

Church (various ones, local)   _____

Additional church   _____

(Other)   _____

Suicide Threat or Attempt

Suicide Hotline   _____

Suicide prevention center   _____

Mental health clinic   _____

Psychiatrist, Psychologist,
or other mental health person   _____

Hospital (local)   _____

(Other)   _____

STEPS IN REFERRING

1. Be familiar with community resources so you can refer to the most appropriate place and/or person.

2. Before referring, check with the referral source to be certain that your helpee can be accepted for help.

3. Tell your helpee why you feel he or she needs to be referred.

4. Indicate to the helpee your reason for each particular referral recommendation you've shared with him or her.

5. Try to involve your helpee in the decision to refer.

6. Let your helpee make his or her own appointment, if possible. You may not have the necessary information needed for scheduling the appointment.

7. If warranted, assist the helpee in planning how he or she will get to the appointment, and determine if another person is needed to go along.

8. Keep an interest in the helpee even after he or she has been referred. Be ready to support the helpee during and after the time he or she is seeing a professional. Let the helpee know you care.

MANDATORY REPORTING TO AUTHORITIES

By law, all cases of child abuse must be reported. This includes physical, emotional, or sexual abuse. Do not feel that something happened too long ago to report it. Report the incident no matter when it occurred. Let the authorities determine if it should be pursued.

Suicide, or the intent to do bodily harm, should always be reported to your supervisor and to the person (parent) who is legally responsible for your helpee.

Remember: It is important and O.K. to recognize your limitations when helping someone and to ask for help from your supervisor, another peer helper, or a professional.

CHAPTER 6

COVERING THE ISSUES

SUICIDE

Suicide is the voluntary act of taking one's own life. It represents a failure in communication between the individual and his or her meaningful relationships, together with an inability to cope with the stresses of life.

Suicide is an act of desperation. It truly is a "dropout" from life which is permanent. Suicide is a permanent solution to a temporary problem.

As a peer helper, you need to take every mention of suicide seriously.

Adolescent suicide and suicide attempts constitute a major problem in the United States today. The present suicide rate for young people has doubled in the last decade and tripled in the last twenty years, while the nation's overall suicide rate has not varied much in the past half-century.

Usually suicidal adolescents are looking at their world through a very narrow perspective.

They say things like, "I've tried everything and nothing works" or "I can't handle it anymore." In reality, they have probably tried very few alternatives. As a peer helper, you will want to enlarge the perspective for these young people and help them find other alternatives.

Stressful Situations That Can Trigger Suicidal Feelings

- Depression which has not been recognized or treated.

- Major life changes, such as death of a parent or friend, school failure, divorce, or breakup with a boyfriend or girlfriend.

- Illness which may be prolonged or terminal.

- Use or abuse of drugs and alcohol.

Facts About Suicide Attempts

- More women than men attempt suicide.

- Men often use more violent methods. Women tend to use barbiturates, other drugs or poisons, while men often use guns.

Facts About Suicides Which are Completed

- More men than women kill themselves.

- Anyone may commit suicide, at any age.

Danger Signs to Look For in the Potentially Suicidal Person

- *Previous attempts* — If the person has attempted suicide before, he or she may be at high risk to try again. The person may talk about previous suicide attempts without saying he or she is considering it at the present time.

- *Threats* — If the helpee is threatening to commit suicide, the peer helper must always take such threats seriously. Experts in the field of suicide estimate that threats are followed by suicide attempts at least seventy percent of the time. The helpee may not say he or she is going to kill himself or herself, but the words may be something like, "I'm not planning to be around much longer."

- *Extreme depression* — If the helpee appears to be extremely depressed or has had changes in personality or behavior, the peer helper will want to look into this further. The helpee's depression may be exhibited by a loss of weight, inability to sleep, or a tendency

to withdraw. Loneliness is a major
factor in suicide.

- *Changes in personality or behavior* — If the
person had been depressed previously,
then all of a sudden seems to be happy
and appears to have had a burden
lifted, the peer helper should probe into
what has happened. Sometimes a
sudden shift in moods may mean that
he or she is relieved because a plan for
suicide has been made. The helpee may
believe the pain of living will soon come
to an end.

- *Preparation for death* — If the helpee is
preparing for death, this is a signal
which should alert the peer helper to
possible danger ahead. The helpee may
start talking about giving away favorite
possessions, making a will, or buying a
gun.

What You Can Do to Help

- *Be alert to what the real problem is.* Listen
to what the helpee is not saying, as well
as to what he or she is saying.

- *Let the person know you take him or her
seriously.*

- *Listen to the person and follow up with
appropriate questions.* If the signs are

apparent, you may ask the person if he or she is thinking about suicide. You may ask if the person has a plan, how that plan would be carried out, and if pills or guns are available. Remember, mentioning suicide does not give the helpee the idea. A suicidal person already has the idea, and talking about it openly may help to prevent the helpee from acting out the suicide.

- *Do not argue or try to reason.* Never tell the helpee, "You can't kill yourself because..."

- *Explore other options with the helpee.* He or she may not realize that other options are available.

- *Tell the person help is available.*

- *Refer the helpee to a professional or a suicide prevention service.* Many people have had extensive training in suicide prevention and are experts in the field.

- *Stay close to the person until professional help is available.*

Common Misconceptions About Suicide

- **False:** If someone wants to kill himself or herself, you can't stop it from happening.

  True: Most suicidal gestures or attempts are a cry for help, which the person cannot communicate by other means.

- **False:** People who talk about killing themselves seldom do.

  True: The majority of persons attempting suicide have talked about it. Suicide threats and attempts must be taken seriously.

- **False:** The tendency toward suicide is inherited and passed on from one generation to another.

  True: Suicide does not "run in families." It has no genetic quality.

- **False:** The suicidal person wants to die and feels there is no turning back.

  True: Suicidal persons most often reveal

ambivalence about living versus dying
and frequently call for help
immediately following the suicide
attempt.

- **False:** Only a certain type of person
  commits suicide.

  True: Suicide occurs in all social classes,
  races, religions, in all personality types
  and all levels of intelligence.

- **False:** Everyone who commits suicide is
  depressed.

  True: Although depression is often
  associated with suicidal feelings, not all
  people who kill themselves are
  obviously depressed. Some of these
  people are anxious, agitated, psychotic,
  or simply feel they can not deal with
  their life situation and want to escape.

- **False:** Suicidal persons rarely seek
  medical help.

  True: In retrospective studies of people
  who had committed suicide, more than

half had sought medical help within the six months preceding the suicide.

- **False:** If you ask a helpee directly, "Do you feel like killing yourself?" that will lead him or her to make a suicide attempt.

  True: Asking a helpee directly about suicidal intent will often minimize the anxiety surrounding the feeling and act as a deterrent to the suicidal behavior.

- **False:** A suicide attempt means that person will always think of attempting it again.

  True: Often a suicide attempt is made during a particularly stressful period. If the remainder of that period is appropriately managed, the person will go on with his or her life.

- **False:** It takes courage for a person to commit suicide.

  True: Suicide is often considered the only way to relieve the pain. It is not an act of courage, but an act of desperation.

Remember: Be alert and listen. Someone may be talking about suicide and you could possibly be the only one who will hear the cry for help.

SELF-ESTEEM

Self-esteem is a feeling of personal self-worth. People who have high self-esteem feel good about themselves, while those with low self-esteem usually find life to be unfulfilling.

As a peer helper, you will want to support your helpees in developing confidence and courage to face their situations. Many problems which will be presented to you will result from the person having low self-esteem. Any way you can help the person to raise his or her self-esteem will fortify the helpee against future potential problems. However, this process must come from within each individual. It is not derived from external sources. No one can create this experience except the individual himself. You, as a peer helper, can be there to listen and support while the process is taking place.

The importance of supporting a helpee in his or her goal to raise self-esteem cannot be overstated. Healthy self-esteem gives a person the ability to respond to the opportunities of life in an active and positive way. You can make a difference in someone's life by helping that person realize how important self-worth really is.

CHILD ABUSE

Child abuse is an act of non-accidental injury or any omission or commission which interferes with a child's development. Child abuse usually means physical injuries inflicted on children by their caretakers; however, it also means emotional abuse. Child neglect is failure of the caretakers to provide adequate nurturing, protection or supervision. Child molesting refers to sexual abuse of children by adults.

Types of Child Abuse

- *Physical abuse* — an act that does harm to a child's body. It may result in bruises, burns, fractures or dislocations, or internal injuries.

- *Emotional abuse* — a verbal act which damages a child's mental and emotional health. This may be done by belittling, screaming, threatening, blaming, or using sarcasm.

- *Sexual abuse* — an act of sexually mistreating a child, either directly by forcing or coercing sexual contact with a child, or indirectly through exposure to pornography.

The Abused Child May Try to Cope by:

- *Being Passive* — He or she will maintain a low profile by trying to stay out of sight. This child hopes to avoid contact with his or her parents and may also avoid other adults, thinking they may be abusive too.

- *Being Responsible* — Older children may take on parenting roles. They will take care of the younger children and do the cooking and cleaning on a regular basis.

- *Being Disruptive* — This child cannot seem to get along with peers or adults. He or she may be aggressive and get into fights often. This person may intentionally provoke adults and get them angry because it is the only way he or she knows how to interact with others.

Example of a State Law

The following is an excerpt from the California Child Abuse Law (Statute: California Penal Code §11161.5).

Definition of a Child: Any person under the age of 18 years.

Nature of Injuries That Must Be Reported: (1) Physical injury or injuries which appear to have been inflicted by other than accidental means by any person: (2) sexual molestation: (3) injuries suffered as a result of any person who, under circumstances or conditions likely to produce great bodily harm or death, or under circumstances other than those likely to produce great bodily harm or death, willfully caused or permitted any child to suffer; or, who inflicted thereon unjustifiable pain or mental suffering; or, having the care or custody of any child, willfully caused or permitted the person or health of such child to have been injured; or, willfully caused or permitted such child to be placed in such situation that its person or health was endangered.

What You Can Do

- *Listen patiently* — Remember the abused person will have feelings of guilt, shame, and helplessness. He or she may be hesitant to admit the abuse because there is a feeling that somehow the abuse is his or her fault.

- *Support the abused person* — He or she may feel guilty about what has happened and also helpless to change the situation.

- *Be nonjudgmental* — Show empathy and concern.

- *Refer to proper mental health professionals* — Because of the emotional trauma of any abuse, the helpee will probably need long-term professional help.

- *Report all abuse or suspected abuse to the proper authorities* — We suggest you first discuss this with your supervisor.

Remember: As a peer helper, you will report all suspicions of child abuse.

FAMILY PROBLEMS

For family problems, we cover divorce, parent/child communication breakdown, and conflict with stepparents. These are only a few of the issues which may be experienced by teens and their families. They have been simplified for better understanding. Many problems are interconnected, and each is unique to the individual. Even though we discuss only three of the many family issues which exist, you will have a good foundation to deal with any other problems that a helpee may bring to you.

Divorce

When someone's family is getting a divorce, the most important thing a peer helper can do is listen. The helpee will have many painful and conflicting feelings. These feelings need to be addressed and released for the helpee to begin the healing process. Your main function is to listen lovingly and to offer support.

A large percentage of peer helpers have experienced a divorce in their family. In this capacity, if you are from a divorced family, you will be able to relate to the feelings expressed and may want to share some of your own experience and feelings on a limited basis. Remember you are there to give your undivided attention to the helpee. Be selective in choosing times to share your own feelings. Letting the helpee know he or she is not alone or different can be very therapeutic—just remember to use your discretion.

Whether or not you have personally felt the pains of divorce, your support for the helpee will be extremely helpful to him or her. What this person needs most is someone to listen, someone who is available for him or her.

Feelings and characteristics to be aware of while helping teenagers who are going through a family separation:

- *Anger* — They are losing something meaningful to them. Anger may be at one parent or both parents. Remember, anger is always an indication of pain.

- *Hurt* — The family is breaking up. A parent is leaving the teenager, and family unity is being severed. The divorce is not just happening to the parents.

- *Loneliness* — Often teenagers are ignored by their parents during this time. Many parents, because of the pain they are experiencing, do not consider the pain the children are going through.

- *Confusion* — They are experiencing the agony of balancing their loyalty to each parent.

- *Disillusionment* — They wonder: Why is this happening? What went wrong? Why me?

- *Isolation* — This is a reaction from the upset in family life and thus their personal life. A tendency to isolate themselves from family and friends is common. Teenagers experiencing divorce in their family may not want to open up about how they are feeling. They may not allow others into their personal world of confusion and pain.

- *Guilt* — Teenagers often assume responsibility for the divorce.

- *Stress* — Teenagers already have a lot of stress. The added strain of divorce may be more than they can handle.

- *Low self-worth* — This becomes an issue particularly if they feel responsible for the divorce. They feel as though they are not "worth" enough for their parents to keep the family together; somehow they are at fault.

Parent/Child Communication Breakdown

"My parents just don't understand."

"You're just a kid; you aren't mature enough yet."

These expressions are classic examples symptomatic of communication breakdown between teens and their parents. When communication is not open and free in a family setting, when yelling or just not talking is the norm, the result is an extremely unhealthy environment. This environment may be the reason for a teen experiencing school problems, feeling angry or depressed, abusing alcohol and other drugs, or acting out rebelliously. Once these problems have surfaced, the lack of healthy communication in a family will serve as a catalyst, making the problems worse.

Usually a helpee will not approach you for help specifically because of a communication problem with his or her parents. Many teenagers may not recognize there is a communication problem in their family because this is what they have lived with all of their life. You will discover that communication breakdown in the family is often an underlying symptom of another issue. Unfortunately, lack of good communication is almost an epidemic when it comes to teens and parents. Neither the teen nor the parent is to blame, although each is responsible for his or her own behavior.

Support you may offer teens who are suffering from communication breakdown with their parents:

- Listen.

- Help the helpee explore the option of learning how to send effective messages.

- Role play a family situation, allowing the helpee to be both the teen and the parent. This allows the helpee to view his or her behavior from a new perspective, and to see how he or she contributes to the family dynamics. The helpee will also be able to better understand where his or her parents are coming from. Role playing will help prepare the helpee for communication situations and hopefully for confronting the parents about how he or she is feeling.

- Assist the helpee in understanding the importance of taking care of himself or herself. The helpee needs to see what

changes need to be made in his or her
own communication skills and behavior.

- Check in with the helpee on a regular
  basis to talk about any progress being
  made. Help the helpee examine what he
  or she could have done differently and
  provide positive reinforcement. It is
  important for the helpee to receive
  affirmation for what he or she is doing
  and encouragement for the risks being
  taken.

- Problems which coincide with the
  communication breakdown also need to
  be addressed. Often it is too unclear to
  know which problem caused the other
  to exist. Many times these problems
  overlap; you and the helpee will need to
  decide which one to work on.

Conflict with Stepparents

When parents get remarried, sometimes the
children resent the stepparent. They may feel as
though the stepparent is an intruder into their
family unit. Or they may feel as if the stepparent
is trying to be "Mom" or "Dad."

Suggestions for the peer helper:

- *Listen to the helpee, using your active listening skills.*

- *Express caring and acceptance.*

- *Role play.* Support the helpee in expressing what he or she is feeling toward the parents and the stepparent. Role playing will assist the helpee in clarifying and working on his or her feelings.

- *Work on how to send effective messages.* The helpee needs to recognize his or her behavior which contributes to conflict with the stepparent.

- *Set objectives and goals with the helpee.* An example of this is the use of sending effective messages in communicating with the stepparent and/or parents about how he or she is feeling.

DEATH AND DYING

Death touches every person at some time or another, and in your role as a peer helper, you will be called upon to be available for a helpee who has experienced such a loss. If the death is in the family, the helpee may not want to talk to other family members, thinking he or she might put an added burden on them. A peer helper can play an important role for the helpee at this time.

Facts About Grief

- The experience of grief is felt by every person at some point during a lifetime.

- Grief is an experience of anxiety and depravation which can manifest itself physically, emotionally, socially, and spiritually.

- Any loss can bring about grief: death of another person, divorce, death of a pet, retirement from one's job, selling a home, or moving away from friends and neighbors.

- Whenever a part of life is removed, there is grief.

Stages of Grief

Granger Westburg, the author of *Good Grief*, has identified several stages of grief. These stages may overlap and merge with each other:

- shock
- emotional release
- depression/loneliness
- physical distress

- panic

- guilt

- hostility/resentment

- inability to return to usual activities

- gradual hope

- struggles to affirm reality

Ways You Can Help the Person Who is Grieving

- Encourage discussion about death before it occurs.

- Be available after the person returns from the funeral and after everyone else has gone. Oftentimes many people are available at the funeral and for the next week thereafter. Usually by the second week friends are back to their normal routines, and the person who is grieving is alone. This is when the peer helper may be most needed.

- Make it known that expressing feelings is good and acceptable. However, do not pressure the griever to show feelings.

- Expect the griever to be emotionally upset and let him or her know you are still available.

- Be a receptive listener.

- Provide practical help in the beginning. Free the person, allowing him or her to have time to grieve.

- Participate in grieving rituals, such as funerals or memorial services.

You may learn that the helpee has found out that he or she has a terminal illness. Because peers feel comfortable talking to peers, you may be the one to whom the dying person reaches out. In order to best relate to this person, you need to know and understand what he or she may be feeling and experiencing.

Fears the Dying Person May Have

- *The fear of the unknown.* The helpee may wonder if "this is all there is" or if there is a life beyond this one.

- *The fear of losing the opportunities and goals of a lifetime.* When young people find out they will not be able to live their life out fully, they often feel a loss and sometimes feel cheated out of what might have been.

- *The fear that after they are dead everyone will get along fine without them.* A young girl may want to talk about her sister moving into her room after she is gone;

a boy may want to talk about his younger brother taking his place on the football team. Feeling that someone will take their place and they will not be missed is a real fear for many people.

- *The fear of pain.* The helpee may be wondering how much pain will come before death. His or her own ability to withstand pain also may be a concern.

- *The fear of being left alone.* The helpee may wonder if the family will have time to make frequent hospital visits. Will death come when no one else is there?

Stages of Death and Dying

In her book *On Death and Dying,* Elizabeth Kubler-Ross talks about the stages a dying person may go through before the end of life. The peer helper should know these stages:

1. *Denial* — The person may refuse to believe that he or she is dying. This stage may vary in length, with some people staying in it longer than others. It is a temporary stage, but it may surface again at any time.

2. *Anger* — The helpee may question why this is happening. When the answer is not apparent, he or she may lash out in anger at the seeming unfairness of it all.

At the same time, the helpee may feel guilty for feeling angry.

3. *Bargaining* — This is usually an attempt to postpone death. The peer helper may not be aware of this stage, since the dying person often does not tell anyone. The bargaining is usually done in secret, often with God.

4. *Depression* — When the dying person faces the reality of his or her death, depression often sets in. It may come when symptoms of terminal illness become impossible to ignore. The helpee may express to the peer helper his or her feelings of despair.

5. *Acceptance* — When the dying person works through the feelings and conflicts that have arisen, he or she may now be ready to accept the fact that death will soon come. The peer helper will recognize this as being a time of emotional calm. The helpee will have reached a state of peace.

What You Can Do for the Dying Person

- *Spend time with the person.* Because this may take more time than is normally spent with each helpee, the peer helper should be careful not to overextend himself or herself. This may include limiting the number of people you help.

- *Listen patiently.* The helpee may want to talk through many different issues.

- *Avoid reacting negatively to the helpee during the anger stage.* Some days the helpee may appear to be angry and may direct that feeling toward the peer helper. By realizing anger is a normal feeling for a dying person, the peer helper should not take the words personally.

- *Explore options with the helpee.* Sometimes the person may feel there are no options available in the months ahead. When he or she has realized options do exist in the life that is left (e.g., deciding to stay at home rather than returning to the hospital), the acceptance of death will be easier.

- *Let the helpee know you care.* Having the knowledge that someone cares and is there for him or her will make a difference to most people.

EATING DISORDERS

Why are we discussing eating disorders? Because it is a serious issue among teenagers, particularly young women. It has always been present, but not until recently has more been revealed about this disorder: the incredible extent of the problem, the acceptance from society that it is real and very serious, and the steps one can take to recover.

Individuals with an eating disorder think that if they could lose weight everything would be better. They lose perspective on how they really appear. They have an image of themselves different from how others see them.

At first, the individual with an active eating disorder is happy about how he or she appears. The person will become more self-confident in school and social activities. As the eating disorder progresses, the individual increasingly focuses on weight and control of food. What follows is lowered self-esteem, isolation, lack of communication with family and friends, and other symptoms which are listed below. Remember, a person need not exhibit all of these symptoms to qualify as having an eating disorder.

What Is an Eating Disorder?

An eating disorder can be described as an abnormal eating pattern, usually resulting from emotional or psychological problems which may produce serious physiological consequences.

Types of Eating Disorders

- *Anorexia nervosa* — self-induced starvation. People with anorexia nervosa have a fear of eating. They have a distorted view of their appearance. These individuals may feel they are fat when in reality they are very thin. Anorexia nervosa is an extremely dangerous eating disorder and can result in death.

- *Bulimia (bulimarexia)* — binging and purging for weight control. Individuals with bulimia eat large amounts of food uncontrollably and eliminate it through vomiting, diuretics, or laxatives. They view their behavior as a way to enjoy food without experiencing weight gain. This develops into a very serious dependency involving much more than weight consciousness.

- *Overeating* — eating compulsively to escape reality and numb feelings. The overeater is using food to "fix it." This

disorder is similar to other obsessive
compulsive disorders.

Symptoms of Eating Disorders

**Characteristics associated with eating
disorders:**

- over-achievement
- perfectionism

Behavior associated with eating disorders:

- preoccupation with food
- unusual eating patterns
- isolation after meals
- obsessive behavior
- social isolation, withdrawal
- drop in grades

Feelings associated with eating disorders:

- low self-worth
- depression
- irritability
- anxiety
- radical mood and personality changes
- inability to concentrate

- not verbalizing thoughts and feelings as often as usual

Obvious physical symptoms associated with eating disorders:

- rapid weight loss or gain
- unattractively and unhealthily thin
- protruding hips
- eyes are watery, bloodshot, and/or have circles
- broken blood vessels in facial area, which results from vomiting
- red, dry cracked lips
- gum chewing, to cover up the smell from vomiting

Not-as-obvious physical symptoms associated with eating disorders:

- dry mouth
- susceptibility to colds
- constipation
- irregular menstrual periods
- weakness and fatigue
- laxative dependence

Steps You Can Take for Helping Someone with an Eating Disorder

1. When the helpee is in denial about his or her disorder and you are recognizing serious symptoms, talk to your supervisor. Eating disorders pose dangerous health threats and should not be minimized or ignored.

2. Remember to use your active listening skills.

3. Assist the helpee in looking at the effects of his or her disorder. If the helpee is in denial, he or she may become defensive. Use your judgment and keep in mind the detrimental effects of eating disorders.

4. When the helpee has admitted to having a problem, listen to the feelings expressed.

5. Let the helpee know there is help and that he or she is not alone.

6. Discuss the options for recovery with the helpee.

7. Ask what he or she would like to do.

8. Make the appropriate referral.

Where to Refer the Helpee

- Overeaters Anonymous — for an overeater, bulimic, or anorexic

- Weight-loss program

- Hospital unit specializing in eating disorders — primarily for an anorexic or bulimic

- Eating disorder specialist (any known professional specializing in eating disorders)

- Counselor, psychologist, psychotherapist, or psychiatrist

SCHOOL PROBLEMS

Many of the helpees who come to you will be experiencing school problems. The primary problem could be related to school or the result of another issue. School problems may include a number of things: attendance, tardiness, grades, a conflict with teachers, or a rebellious attitude toward school and authority in general. Most likely it will be a combination of two or more problems.

Clarifying and specifying the problem is essential when working with a helpee with school troubles. When a student is having problems, the situation tends to be confusing and unclear to him or her. The student often feels overwhelmed;

when an individual is struggling in one area at school, all other areas will be affected. This causes tremendous stress and feelings of hopelessness.

You may be able to direct the helpee to focus on a specific problem in order to create an actual starting point for working on his or her situation. This will help relieve some of the stress the helpee is experiencing.

Keep in mind that troubles in school are often an indicator of another underlying problem, for example, family problems, alcohol and drug use, or low self-esteem.

Steps to Follow When Working with the Helpee on School Problems

1. Define the problem.

> → Ask the helpee what he or she feels the problem is.

> → Work with the helpee to clarify the specific problem(s). For example, if the problem is in a certain class, have the helpee pinpoint exactly what is troubling to him or her.

> → Use your active listening skills, which will be essential in aiding the helpee to define the problem.

2. Make up a plan.

→ Specify an area of school performance to work on (e.g., attendance, grades).

→ With the helpee, establish a realistic goal he or she would like to achieve.

→ Establish short-term objectives as part of the plan; for example, the helpee will attend English five days in a row or will turn in a specific assignment on time.

→ Discuss and write down the steps to take in achieving the established goal. It is important that the student not take on too much at once. Small, gradual steps may be necessary to build self-confidence and to prevent the student from becoming discouraged and giving up.

→ Discuss how often, where, and at what time you and the helpee will meet to check progress and talk about how the helpee is feeling.

3. Discuss the outcome.

→ Have the helpee discuss the pros and the cons of his or her present behavior and of the goal which has been established.

→ Have the helpee discuss what behavior he or she wants to change.

4. Check helpee's progress.

→ Give positive reinforcement for the progress the helpee has made.

→ Offer support and empathy.

PEER PRESSURE

Much of the social pressure teens receive comes from people who attend school with them. Peer pressure causes teens to do things they do not want to do, but they will do them to be "one of the crowd," to fit in, to feel liked and accepted. One of the most typical situations is when other teens pressure another into drinking or using other drugs. Another common peer pressure problem is teens being pressured into having sex.

The unfortunate thing about peer pressure situations is that it is often the beginning of a cycle, not just a one-time incident. Once teens have been pressured into doing something they do not feel right about, it becomes less difficult the following time to repeat the behavior. Soon they will be the ones pressuring a peer. This is not true of all peer pressure situations, but it is extremely common.

How to Assist a Helpee
in Working Through Peer Pressure

- Let the helpee know he or she is special. It is important to reinforce the unique and likable qualities the helpee has.

- Work with the helpee on clarifying his or her values. This will aid the helpee in drawing boundaries between what others value and what he or she truly wants for himself or herself.

- Support the helpee in building his or her self-esteem. Each person must gain self-esteem to have a better sense of doing what he or she wants, instead of trying to please others in order to feel good about himself or herself. When someone acts against his or her own values and beliefs in order to be accepted, the person's self-esteem is never built up, only cheated.

- Work with the helpee on being assertive so that in a peer pressure situation he or she can learn to:

  → express what he or she wants to do

  → express how he or she feels about the situation

→ be honest, using a firm and direct
tone

→ be respectful of others in the
situation

→ be spontaneous in expressing
feelings, trying not to hesitate

→ accept responsibility for the
feelings expressed

- Role play with the helpee, emphasizing
assertive techniques (the ones
mentioned above are only a few
suggestions; do not close the door on
any other ideas). Remember to reinforce
the helpee's own values.

- Remind the helpee that no one will
ostracize him or her for doing what he
or she feels is best. If anything, the
helpee may discover that his or her new
behavior will elicit respect. If not, the
other people involved obviously have
some issues to work on themselves.

Remember: You will frequently encounter helpees with school problems. Experience will serve
to be a useful tool. You will be able to offer
empathy and support. Trust your instincts and
listen!

SUBSTANCE ABUSE

The term "substance abuse" encompasses the use of both alcohol and drugs. Most teenagers experiment with these substances; some of these teens may develop a temporary problem; others will not like the effects; and some will become addicted. Alcoholism is a disease. Young as well as older people become afflicted with it.

During your experience as a peer helper, you likely will find students coming to you with school-related problems or feelings of depression. Many of these teenagers actually have a more serious underlying problem: substance abuse.

Substance abuse may be either the cause or result of other problems. Whatever the situation is, the problem with alcohol and drugs must be dealt with first. The student with a substance abuse problem will experience difficulty in all areas of his or her life: school, friendships, relationships, family, and health.

Sometimes a student may approach you, already having surrendered to the fact that he or she has a substance abuse problem. In this case, the helpee has overcome denial, which is the most deadly factor in alcoholism and drug addiction. You will be able to listen to the helpee's feelings and explain his or her options.

Symptoms of substance abuse are not the same for each person. There are many unique situations and variations according to the individual. Remember to use your active listening skills and go to your supervisor with any questions or doubts.

Categories of Drugs

Depressants

Depressants slow down or reduce physiological functions.

Common drugs abused	Street name(s)
Alcohol	Booze
Barbiturates	Downers, reds, barbs
Tranquilizers	Valium, Librium, Xanax (brand names)
Marijuana	Pot, weed, grass, bud joint, reefer, smoke
Hashish	Hash
Methaqualone	Ludes, quads

Stimulants

Stimulants speed up or increase physiological functions.

Common drugs abused	Street name(s)
Amphetamines	Speed, whites, uppers
Methamphetamine	Meth, speed, go-fast, go, zip, chris, christy, crank, crystal
Chrystal Methamphetamine	Ice, quartz, glass, crack meth, ice cream, Shabu (Japanese), Kaksonjae and Hiropon (Korean), Batu (Filipino)
Cocaine	Coke, crack, blow, snow, white
Nicotine	Cigarettes

Hallucinogenics

Hallucinogens and psychedelics cause major distortion of thoughts and senses. They produce a psychosis-like state of mind, characterized by visual hallucinations.

Common drugs abused	Street name(s)
Lysergic acid deithylamide	LSD, acid, L, love drug
Psilocybin	magic mushrooms, 'shrooms
Phencyclidine	PCP, angel dust
Methylenedioxy-methamphetamine (MDMA)	Ecstasy, X, Adam, Eve, Mickey Mouse
Mescaline	
Peyote	

Narcotics

Opiates or narcotic analgesics decrease pain. Use of these results in euphoria, decrease in breathing rate, pain relief, and physical dependence.

Common drugs abused	Street name(s)
Morphine	Morphine
Methylmorphine	Codeine
Diacetylmorphine	Heroin
Meperidine	Demerol
Propoxyphene	Darvon

Physical Symptoms/Indicators of Substance Abuse

- alcohol on breath
- sudden weight loss or gain
- poor complexion
- hyperactivity
- sluggishness
- change in pupil size
- sleep disturbances
- rapid speech
- shakiness
- red/irritable nasal area

Symptoms Resulting or Relating Directly from Abuse

- increase in use
- dependency
- inability to control use
- change in the type of substance used
- preoccupation with drugs and alcohol
- blackouts

- serious consequences from use (i.e., drunk driving or drunk-in-public arrests)

- memory loss

- rapid mood changes

Personality Characteristics and Feelings

- mood swings

- depression

- anger

- unreliability

- irritability

- defensiveness

- lying

- isolation

Symptoms Relating to School, Friends, and Social Habits

- change in peer group

- change in dress or grooming habits

- drop in attendance at school

- drop in grades

- change in financial status

- rebellious attitude and delinquent acting out

- loss of interest in school or extracurricular activities

Steps You Can Take When the Helpee is in Denial

1. Assist the helpee in looking at the effect of the substance abuse on his or her life.

2. Work with the helpee in defining the problem.

3. When serious consequences are occurring, talk to your peer helping supervisor.

Steps You Can Take When the Helpee Has Admitted a Substance Abuse Problem

1. Discuss options for recovery.

2. Ask the helpee what he or she wants to do.

3. Make an appropriate referral.

Where to Refer the Helpee

- Alcoholics Anonymous

- Narcotics Anonymous

- Cocaine Anonymous

- A recovering alcoholic/addict you know personally or through your peer helping class

- A substance abuse program at your school (not all schools have this)

- A counselor, psychologist, psychotherapist, or psychiatrist—preferably one who works with alcoholics/addicts regularly.

- Drug and alcohol dependency unit—inpatient.

- Drug and alcohol dependency center—outpatient.

Things to Keep in Mind

- Always deal with the helpee's feelings.

- You will be unable to successfully work with the helpee on any other issues while he or she is still abusing alcohol and drugs.

- The substance abuser will feel hopeless, powerless, and frustrated in his or her life. The person may feel there is no way to change him- or herself or the life situations around him or her.

TEENAGE PREGNANCY

The United States is experiencing an epidemic of teen pregnancies—more than any other industrialized nation. This epidemic's results for teenagers include poverty, curtailed education, and greater physical risks for the young mother and her child.

Facts about Teenage Pregnancy

Source: U.S. Department of Health and Human Services

- Four out of every ten teenage girls will become pregnant at least once before they are twenty years old.

- The younger the mother, the more likely she is to have complications from pregnancy. These might include anemia, toxemia, or a miscarriage.

- The younger the mother, the more likely her baby will have a low birth weight, which is a major cause of infant mortality. Her baby also is more likely to suffer from birth defects and mental retardation than the baby who is born to a woman who is older.

- Only half of all teen mothers finish high school.

- Teen mothers who marry are three times more likely to be separated or divorced within 15 years than are the women who wait until they are in their twenties to have children.

- Two-thirds of families headed by teen mothers exist below the poverty level.

As a peer helper, you may be called upon to help young women who are pregnant or who think they are. You must deal with your own feelings on this issue in order to remain objective. If you are not comfortable with the issue of pregnancy, you may choose to refer the helpee to a different peer helper.

Considerations When Helping Pregnant Teens

- The helpee may have conflicting feelings.

- The helpee often does not know what to do.

- She may reach out to you for assistance and support.

- Remember to assist the helpee in dealing with her feelings.

- Encourage the helpee to reach out to other people in her life for support.

- You may want to refer the helpee to the school counselor, mental health professional, or minister for further guidance and an exploration of options.

CHAPTER 7

MOTIVATION

Becoming a peer helper is like any other new experience. It is exciting, challenging, interesting, and rewarding. This initial thrill may not last indefinitely. There may come times when you are tired, depressed, burned-out, or unmotivated. Do not feel guilty. Your feelings are perfectly normal. You may need some time away from helpees. During your rest period, take time for yourself. You may use this time to regroup and revitalize— and to see where you are with your own feelings.

During your time of reflection, concentrate on your successes, not on your apparent failures. Situations which may have seemed unsuccessful to you may have planted seeds which will blossom sometime in the future. You may hear about them later, or you may never know the important contribution you have made to someone's life. Just keep in mind that the more helpees you see, the more successes you will have—and by the law of statistics, more failures also. Professional counselors recognize the fact that they cannot help everyone they see. They know they will have some failures. You will also have some failures. Do not feel guilty about them. Do the very best job you can do; refer to a professional when you cannot handle a situation; and feel good about what you have accomplished.

You, the peer helper, are a very special person. You fill a spot which is unique. Other people will come to you for help because they will recognize those qualities in you which they admire and respect. They will see your concern and caring for people of all races, economic status and cultural heritage. You will be recognized as a nonjudgmental person who does not stereotype a person because of his or her physical appearances, abilities, values, or ethnic origins. Your dedication and endurance for sticking with a helpee through "thick and thin" will be noticed and appreciated. You will model certain behavior which you will want to see developed in your helpee—he or she will see the respect you have for yourself and the value you place on your own high self-esteem. You will radiate the love you have for all people who are experiencing many kinds of problems and life situations.

In summary, you are a peer helper because you care and are concerned; you accept and do not judge; you show dedication and endurance; you model self-awareness and high self-esteem; you radiate love. How fortunate your helpee is to have you as a peer helper. How special you are!

Listen

*When I ask you to listen to me and you start giving
advice, you have not done what I asked.*

*When I ask you to listen to me and you begin to tell me
why I shouldn't feel that way,
you are trampling on my feelings.*

*When I ask you to listen to me and you feel you have to
do something to solve my problem,
you have failed me, strange as that may seem.*

*Listen!! All I asked, was that you listen.
Not to talk or do—just hear me.*

*Advice is cheap; 10 cents will get both Dear Abby and
Billy Graham in the same newspaper.*

And I can do for myself; I'm not helpless.

*But, when you accept as a simple fact that I do feel what I
feel no matter how irrational, then I can quit trying to
convince you and get about the business of understanding
what's behind this irrational feeling. And when that's
clear, the answers are obvious and I don't need advice.*

*Irrational feelings make sense when we understand
what's behind them.*

*Perhaps that's why prayer works, sometimes,
for people because God is mute,
and he doesn't give advice or try to fix things.
He just listens and lets you work it out for yourself.*

*So please, listen and just hear me. And, if you want to
talk, wait a minute for your turn; and I'll listen to you.*

—Anonymous

BIBLIOGRAPHY

Alberti, Robert E., Ph.D., and Michael L. Emmons, Ph.D. *Your Perfect Right: A Guide to Assertive Living.* San Luis Obispo, California: Impact Publishers, 1985.

Anonymous. *Alcoholics Anonymous.* New York: Alcoholics Anonymous World Services, Inc., 1987.

Boskind-White, M., and W. C. White, Jr. *Bulimarexia, The Binge/Purge Cycle.* New York: W. W. Norton and Company, 1988.

Bower, Sharon, and Gordon Bower. *Asserting Yourself.* Reading, Massachusetts: Addison-Wesley, 1976.

Brammer, Lawrence. *The Helping Relationship: Process and Skills.* Englewood Cliffs, New Jersey: Prentice-Hall, 1973.

Bruch, H. *The Golden Cage: The Enigma of Anorexia Nervosa.* Cambridge, Massachusetts: Harvard University Press, 1978.

Carkhuff, Robert R. *The Art of Helping VI.* Amherst, Massachusetts: Human Resource Development Press, Inc., 1987.

Carroll, Charles R. *Drugs in Modern Society*. Dubuque, Iowa: Wm. C. Brown Publishers, 1985.

D'Andrea, Vincent, and Peter Salovey. *Peer Counseling Skills and Perspectives*. Palo Alto, California: Science and Behavior Books, 1983.

Egan, Gerald. *You and Me: The Skills of Communicating and Relating To Others*. Monterey, California: Brooks/Cole Publishing Company, 1977.

Egan, Gerald. *The Skilled Helper*, third edition. Monterey, California: Brooks/Cole Publishing Company, 1986.

Furstenberg, F., Jr., J. Menken, and R. Lincoln. *Teenage Sexuality, Pregnancy, and Childbearing*. Philadelphia: University of Pennsylvania Press, 1981.

Garfinkel, P. E., and D. M. Garner. *Anorexia Nervosa: A Multidimensional Perspective*. New York: Brunner/Mazel, 1982.

Gray, H.D., and J. Tindall. *Peer Counseling: In-depth Look at Training Peer Helpers*. Muncie, Indiana: Accelerated Development, 1985.

Johnston, L. D., J. G. Bachman, and P. M. O'Malley. *Highlights from Student Drug Use in America 1975-1981*. U.S. Department of Health and Human Services, Public Health Service, National Institute on Drug Abuse, 1982.

Kennedy, Eugene. *Crisis Counseling: The Essential Guide for Nonprofessional Counselors*. New York: Continuum Publishing Company, 1986.

Kubler-Ross, Elizabeth. *On Death and Dying*. New York: MacMillan Publishing Company, 1969.

Kubler-Ross, Elizabeth. *AIDS: The Ultimate Challenge.* New York: MacMillan Publishing Company, 1987.

Levenkron, S. *Treating and Overcoming Anorexia Nervosa.* New York: Warner Books, 1982.

Loughary, W. John, and Theresa M. Ripley. *Helping Others Help Themselves.* New York: McGraw-Hill, 1979.

MacFarlane, Kee, and Jill Waterman with Shawn Conerly, Linda Damon, Michael Durfee, and Suzanne Long. *Sexual Abuse of Young Children.* New York: Guilford Publications, Inc., 1986.

Moore, Joseph. *A Teen's Guide to Ministry.* Liguori, Missouri: Liguori Publications, 1988.

Myrick, Robert D., and Tom Ervey. *Caring and Sharing.* Minneapolis, Minnesota: Educational Media Corporation, 1984.

Myrick, Robert D., and Tom Ervey. *Youth Helping Youth.* Minneapolis, Minnesota: Educational Media Corporation, 1985.

Myrick, Robert D., and Don L. Sorenson. *Peer Helping: A Practical Guide.* Minneapolis, Minnesota: Educational Media Corporation, 1988.

Peck, M. L. *Youth Suicide.* New York: Springer Publishers, 1985.

Phillips, Maggie. *The Peer Counseling Training Manual.* Revised and expanded by Joan Sturkie. San Jose, California: Resource Publications, Inc., 1991.

Riebel, Linda K., Ph.D. *Understanding Eating Disorders: A Guide for Healthcare Professionals.* Sacramento, California: Robert D. Anderson Publishing Company, 1988.

Rogers, Carl R. *On Becoming A Person*. Boston, Massachusetts: Houghtin-Mifflin Company, 1961.

Satir, Virginia. *Self-Esteem*. Milbrae, California: Celestial Arts, 1975.

Sturkie, Joan. *Listening With Love: True Stories From Peer Counseling*. San Jose, California: Resource Publications, Inc., 1987.

Sturkie, Joan, and Gordon R. Bear. *Christian Peer Counseling: Love In Action*. Dallas, Texas: Word, Inc., 1989.

Sturkie, Joan, and Marsh Cassady. *Acting It Out: 74 Short Plays for Starting Discussions with Teenagers*. San Jose, California: Resource Publications, Inc., 1990.

Sturkie, Joan, and Charles Hanson, PhD. *Leadership Skills for Peer Group Facilitators*. San Jose, California: Resource Publications, Inc., 1992.

Van Cleave, Stephen, Walter Bryd and Kathy Revell. *Counseling for Substance Abuse and Addiction*. Waco, Texas: Word Books, 1987.

Van Ornum, William, and John B. Mordock. *Crisis Counseling With Children and Adolescents: A Guide for Nonprofessional Counselors*. New York: Continuum Publishing Company, 1983.

Varenhorst, Barbara. *Real Friends*. San Francisco: Harper and Row, 1983.

Varenhorst, Barbara with Lee Sparks. *Training Teenagers for Peer Ministry*. Loveland, Colorado: Group Books, 1988.

Wallerstein, J. S., and J. B. Kelly. *Surviving the Breakup: How Children and Parents Cope with Divorce*. New York: Basic Books, 1980.

Be sure your students grow from community-service work.

THE SERVICE VOLUNTEER'S HANDBOOK

Ret Thomas & Dorine Thomas

Paper, 128 pages, 4.25' x 7", ISBN: 0-89390-442-2

If students are not prepared for community service they can walk away with a bad experience or worse. You need to make sure they're ready with the proper skills. Here's a quick personal tool for students that will help make their involvement with community service a rewarding one. The handbook works like a specialized day planner for students. It includes worksheets, planners, an address book, client profile sheets, forms plus special exercises to make sure they grow from their community service. This handbook makes service training a snap.

LOOKING IN, REACHING OUT
A Manual for
Training Service Volunteers

Dorine and Ret Thomas

Looseleaf w/binder, 192 pages, 8.5" x 11", ISBN: 0-89390-376-0

This ready-to-go training course, designed by a school counselor for service volunteers, covers all the basics. With it, you can make sure your adult or youth volunteers feel suited and prepared for helping ministry. Includes handout masters with permission to photocopy. Use it as an activity book for your own meetings or as a formal training course.

Get the discussions started.

FACING VIOLENCE
Discussion-starting Skits for Teenagers

R. William Pike

Paper, 192 pages, 6" x 9", ISBN: 0-89390-344-2

You can get teenagers to talk about their problems by using simple dramas. Facing Violence provides you with 40 skits addressing violence in schools, violence in the home, violent language, violence and dating, violence in society, and solutions to violence. These skits require no rehearsal.

FACING SUBSTANCE ABUSE
Discussion-Starting Skits for Teenagers

R. William Pike

Paper, 6" x 9", 192 pages, ISBN: 0-89390-374-4

Tobacco. Alcohol. Drugs. These substances threaten the lives of teenagers today. The danger comes not only from how they themselves use controlled substances but from the prevalence of abuse among their families and friends. Teenagers need to know how to respond. With these real-to-life skits, which can be performed without props or rehearsal, you can get young people to work out practical ways to respond to the substance abuse in their lives. Contains more than 40 skits which have been developed and tested. They work.

74 Short Plays for Starting
Discussions with Teenagers

ACTING
IT OUT

Joan Sturkie & Marsh Cassady

ACTING IT OUT
74 Short Plays for Starting Discussions With Teenagers

Joan Sturkie and Marsh Cassady, PhD

Paperbound, 358 pages, 6" x 9"
ISBN: 0-89390-178-4

Getting teens to talk about their feelings and personal experiences can be frustrating. *Acting It Out* offers a new approach: Teens act out a short play, then discuss how the characters deal with the particular issue. Questions at the end of each drama help articulate issues and feelings. These dramas address challenging subjects: abortion, suicide, child abuse, gangs, anorexia, home life, drugs. Issues are presented in a straightforward manner and your teens are encouraged to talk about them in the same way.

Discussion Starters for 10-13 Year Olds

ACTING
IT OUT
Junior

Joan Sturkie · Marsh Cassady, PhD

ACTING IT OUT JUNIOR
Discussion Starters for 10-13 Year Olds

Joan Sturkie and Marsh Cassady, PhD

Paperbound, 160 pages, 6" x 9"
ISBN: 0-89390-240-3

This book is similar to the popular *Acting It Out* collection except that these 48 skits address issues important to younger people: abuse, alcoholism in the family, dating, drug abuse, gang activity, homosexuality, cheating, shoplifting, and more.

You can help teens help themselves.

THE PEER HELPING TRAINING COURSE

Joan Sturkie and Maggie Phillips

Looseleaf, 126 pages, 8.5" x 11"
ISBN: 0-89390-311-6

A revised and expanded version of *The Peer Counseling Training Course*, this is a complete curriculum and teacher's guide for a high school course, which can also be used with some junior high school students. Four new chapters have been added to this edition

The Peer Helping Training Course helps teens learn how to be there for each other. The practical training course is divided into two sections. Part one (units 1-9) introduces the skills students need to be good communicators. Part two (units 10-23) deals with specific problems such as peer pressure, drugs, death, and AIDS. Appendices contain a sample letter to parents of peer helpers, glossary, community resourses, and an excellent bibliography.

Peer Helper's Pocket Book Special Bulk Prices

Give a copy to each of your peer helpers and help them better understand their role, the skills they need and the referral information that is so important to what they do.

1-9 copies	$7.95
10-24 copies	$7.15
25-49 copies	$6.36
50-99 copies	$5.57
100-249 copies	$5.41